MORETON WIRRAL

A Pictorial History

Volume I

by

Frank Biddle & Alan Fellowes

First published 1992 by Countyvise Limited, 1 & 3 Grove Road, Rock Ferry, Birkenhead, Wirral, Merseyside L42 3XS, and Metropolitan Borough of Wirral, Central Library, Borough Road, Birkenhead, Wirral L41 2XB.

Copyright © Frank Biddle and Alan Fellowes, 1992.

ISBN 0 907768 56 3. Countyvise Limited.

ISBN 0 904582 14 0 Metropolitan Borough of Wirral Central Library

Photoset and printed by Birkenhead Press Limited, 1 & 3 Grove Road, Rock Ferry, Birkenhead, Merseyside L42 3XS.
Front cover and illustrations designed by Michelle Smith.

The top picture dates from 1927, showing Kerr's Field in flood. The bottom picture is of Hoylake Road about 1900 showing Churchill Farm looking towards Moreton Cross. The farm stretched from Holt Avenue to Rosslyn Drive. The site is now occupied by Barclays Bank, a newsagents and other shops ending with Philip Davies (Estate Agents) on the corner of Rosslyn Drive.

A Short History of Moreton

Moreton was originally known as Moreton-cum-Lingham. Moreton came from an Anglo-Saxon word — More meaning a Lake, Ton meaning Town. It had that name long before the embankment was built as the area between Great Meols, Bidston and the Wallasey slopes was a tidal lagoon — easy to picture as 3,000 acres of Moreton are between 3 and 5 feet below sea level, with most of the remainder not much more than 5 feet above sea level. Lingham comes from the Norse words — Lyng and Holm, Lyng meaning heather and Holm meaning island, thus Heather Island. Leasowe was known as the Leasowes, an Anglo-Saxon word meaning 'meadow pastures'. On a survey map of the parish dated 1665, in the possession of the Vyner family, there is a road leading from Moreton to Lingham called the Lake Way, now called Lingham Lane. There has been known occupation of Lingham, Moreton and Meols going back to Roman times and beyond; as there have been many Roman coins found in the vicinity and other artifacts from earlier times. Moreton has had many ups and downs in its history. It was part of the Parish of Bidston and was the wealthiest and most productive of the lands run for the Birkenhead Priory. By the mid 1800's the area became steadily run down, but with the introduction of the railway in 1866, it brought day trippers from Liverpool and further afield. By 1900, Moreton's reputation was growing in popularity as a place for a healthy holiday — many doctors recommended Moreton for a holiday or as a place to live, with its clean air, sunshine and paddling in the sea to help cure rheumatism and other ailments. Moreton's fame grew so much that it came to the notice of Margaret Beavan and with guidance from the medical profession, she chose Leasowe as the place to build the Liverpool Open-Air Hospital for children with tuberculosis. In 1948 the hospital became known as Leasowe Children's Hospital when the National Health Service came into operation.

Moreton has changed a lot from a population of 165 in 1665 to the present day population of 25,000 and is still growing. The two largest increases in population were after both wars. Between 1911 and 1921 it grew from 898 to 2,531, and between 1941 and 1951, it grew from 5,021 to 7,716. Wallasey, needing more space to expand, obtained powers through an Act of Parliament in 1928 to take over Moreton. Wallasey extended their boundaries again in 1933 to include Saughall Massie, and part of Upton and Bidston. With the introduction of two of the largest firms of their type in the country, namely Cadbury and Squibb, good housing and a good shopping centre that caters for most needs, it looks as though Moreton has shed its past of 'Moreton in the mud' to 'Moreton in a traffic jam'!!!

The picture above shows the unveiling of the Wallasey Boundary sign on the day the Wallasey Boundaries were extended to include Moreton — the date was the 1st April 1928. A Civic Party came by coach and cars to watch the Mayor Dr. John McMillan (he is wearing the top hat in the middle of the picture) unveil the Wallasey sign in Upton Road, Moreton.

Moreton Station was built in 1865 and was first opened for passenger service on June 18th 1866. It was a single track until 1894-5. The line was electrified in 1938 and all the stations were modernised and have changed little up to the present day. It had no Station Master's House. The shelter on the Liverpool side was used by the players of the Moreton Football Club as a changing room in its early days. The pitch was situated roughly where the present day Premier Brands football pitch is now.

Dates of the pictures are: above — 1937; top right — 1909; bottom right — 1920.

205

Moreton Station

The names of the railway workers on this picture, from left to right, are — Jim Dodd, Jack Parr, Tommy Cookson, Alf Mack, Tommy Evans, Stan Wharton and Jack Stanley.

Leasowe Station was built in 1895 when the line was being altered from a single line to a double line track. The Station Master's House was built at the same time and pulled down in 1937 when the line was modernised and electrified. The foot bridge was added much later — in 1947. The man in the picture is Robert O'Leary.

The dates of these pictures are: left — 1903, top — 1910, bottom — 1936, the train in this picture was built by Beyer, Peacock and Company in the early 1900's.

Christ Church, Moreton, was built in 1863 on land donated by Mr. Tom Webster and the money for the building of the church and rectory was donated by Mr. William Inman, the Shipping Magnate of Upton Manor. The picture was taken about 1912 and shows the old oil lamps. The pulpit in the picture was taken away from the left-hand side, and an oak pulpit put in its place on the right-hand side, where it still is now. This all happened in 1958. The family pews of the Inman and Clegg families were removed about 1929 after the installation of electric lights, the wooden bases remain. The choir, then of un-robed men and women, sat in the recess on the left, where the organ is now.

The top-right hand page shows the bell ringers of Christ Church. When they had done their job, they went to the Plough Inn for a drink and returned to ring the bells at the end of the service, they went home without attending the service. This did not go down well with the Vicar and caused a great deal of ill-feeling.

The names of the men in the picture, from left to right are: Jim Stanley, Tommy Potter, Edwin Stanley, Joe Gardiner and in the picture below, dating from the 1910's, you can see the Rectory on the left-hand side, which was pulled down in 1922.

Parish Church, Moreton.   E. Whatling, Moreton.

The picture below is of the first Catholic Church in Moreton. It was built in a field at the bottom of the now Marion Drive, where the Arrowebrook Snooker Club is; during 1922/3 by public subscription, at a cost of £1,200. It was pulled down in 1955 and re-placed by the present day one, situated on the corner of Sandbrook Lane/Hoylake Road. The foundation stone was laid on the 25th June 1955 by the Bishop of Shrewsbury, the Right Reverend John A. Murphy, D.D. It was to cost £42,000.

The lady in the picture below is Miss Kathleen Pitman, it was taken in the summer of 1927. The picture on the right, top, is showing the interior of the old church and also the last wedding to be held there by Father Rees, the couple being Mr. and Mrs. Howlett. The picture, bottom right, is showing the Catholic Day Parade, which was held regularly until the 1950's and started from the Sacred Heart School, along Hoylake Road to the Church. People came from miles around to see the procession and take part. Mr. Conroy, Mr. Brownbill and Mr. O'Connell to name a few that can be seen amongst those leading the parade.

9

The top picture was known as 'Richards Cottage'. It stood opposite Chapelhill Road and was built in the early 1800's. It was used as a small holding until it was pulled down in 1947, for the widening of the road and building of the present day houses.

Below is Dodd's Cottage. It was situated on the right-hand side of the Atlantic Garage and was pulled down in the 1970's when the Provident Cheque Company moved over the road to the corner of Orchard Road — they were the last owners. The foundations are still there. The Dodd family, who were the original owners, were Coal Merchants and Furniture Removers, among many other things. They also had the first telephone in Moreton.

The cottage above was on the site of the present day Co-op on the corner of Holt Avenue. It fell into dis-repair in the 1930's and fell down. The man by the window is Mr. Jack Smith.

The picture below is of Felicity Cottage, built in 1841. It was situated where Felicity Grove is now and pulled down in 1948 to accommodate the building of the present day houses.

The public houses, old and new. The oldest of the three main public houses in Moreton was the Plough Inn and the Druids Arms, dating from the seventeenth century, it is the third building on this site. The Druids Arms part of the name was dropped by the 1930's. The picture dates from the middle 1920's when Mr. Joseph Wharton was the licencee. The picture below shows the new public house on opening day in June 1938, with the barmen standing in the doorways.

The second oldest is the Farmers Arms dating from the late 1700's. The picture above dates from the early 1900's. Part of it was still being used as a farm, namely the building on the right in the top picture. It was used to store hay up until the First World War, when it was given a coat of whitewash and generally cleaned up. The fence with the public house's name on it was moved to this side of the barn. The lady in the doorway of the Farmers Arms is Mrs. Hale, the wife of the licencee, Mr. William Hale.

The picture below dates from 1934 when the new Farmers Arms public house opened.

The youngest of the three public houses is the Coach & Horses, dating from the early 1800's. The picture above dates from the early 1900's, when the licencee was Mrs. Emma Borrowman. In the picture below you can see the old and the new together, the date being 1928, although the old public house was pulled down that year. The three cottages were to stand for two more years; their back gardens are where the extension is now (that was built in the early 1960's. The new Coach & Horses quickly got two nicknames, one being "The Big House" and the other "The Cathedral". The licencee of both old and new Coach & Horses was Mr. Swarbrick.

The top picture is of Pasture Road in the late 1930's. The farm on the right-hand side was Dawson's farm, where the present-day car park and Youth Club are now. The farm was pulled down during the 1960's.

The bottom picture is of an Armistice Day Parade in 1951 outside the present-day British Legion Cenotaph.

Upton Road during the early 1900's. The top picture is looking at the Plantation approximately where the present roundabout is now.

The bottom picture is looking up Upton Road. You can see part of Church Farm on the right where the entrance to Chadwick Street and a row of shops now stand. The houses in the picture were built about 1902. The bay windows were removed in the 1920's and the houses were converted into shops, present day — Foster's, Sayers and Dewhursts.

Upton Road looking towards Moreton Cross in the 1930's. The road was widened and straightened about this time. In the bottom picture, on the left-hand side, stands the old British Legion and Cenotaph. The flag pole can be seen. Later in the mid 1940's it became the first public library in Moreton. During the mid 1950's it was moved to a specially built building in Pasture Road. After the old library was pulled down, two houses and Winston Grove were built. Winston Grove was named after Winston Churchill.

The top picture is of Willaston Road in 1927. The road was built in two parts — the left-hand side was built in 1914, before the Great War and the right-hand side was built in 1918/19 after the war.

The bottom picture is of Silverburn Avenue being built in the early 1900's, as can be seen the work is only two-thirds done.

Clap Lane
Moreton

Both these pictures are of Clap Lane. The one on the left was taken in winter and the one below in summer. Clap Lane is situated in Pasture Road opposite the British Legion, it has no name-plate, it runs down the side of Moreton Library. The elm trees fell to the Dutch Elm disease and the last were finally cut down in the middle 1970's.

A LANE IN MORETON

The top picture is of Pasture Road covered in snow during the winter of 1912. You can see Dial House and Mary Ann's Cottage on the right and the hay stacks covered in snow on the left. The boy in the picture is Andy Beed.

Below is Old Church Farm House — it was being used as a Clinic at that time. You can just see the entrance to Chadwick Street on the left. The Police Hut was there until the early 1950's and was later moved to new purpose-built premises in Chadwick Street in 1955. This picture was taken about 1928.

The top picture shows the entrance to Pasture Road. The corner where the man is standing on the left-hand side, was known as Cart House corner. The small shop on the right was owned by Miss Birch. To enter the shop, you had to go down two steps, and it used to flood after heavy rain.

The picture below is of Hoylake Road about 1929. It shows the Coach & Horses on the left-hand side, the 'island' that to-day stands between the main road and the Coach & Horses, is where the old Coach & Horses and bowling green were. Looking at the picture, the lady with her dog gives you a guide-line to its approximate position. On the right of the picture you can see the vacant site where the T.S.B. Bank and Chemist shops are to-day. They and the rest of the shops on that corner were built in the early 1960's. The last two families to live in the cottages in front of the Coach & Horses were the Hardcastle and Stanley families.

Moreton from the Air.

Ariel photograph of Moreton Cross taken approximately 1924. There are 11 farms and smallholdings in the picture, starting from the left at Sandbrook Lane — Stanley's farm, Smith's farm, Church Farm and almost out of the picture at the top right hand-side, Wilson's farm. On the bottom of the picture, on the right-hand side is Barnston Lane with 3 farms — Bostock's farm, Pear Tree Farm and Old Hall Farm. There was a small-holding at the back of the old Coach & Horses public house. In Pasture Road, on the left-hand side, was Parkinson's farm. At the back of the Picture House, where the Clinic is to-day, is a small-holding. And last but not least, next to the Plough Inn, is Jefferies Cottage and small-holding. There is not a car to be seen in the picture.

22

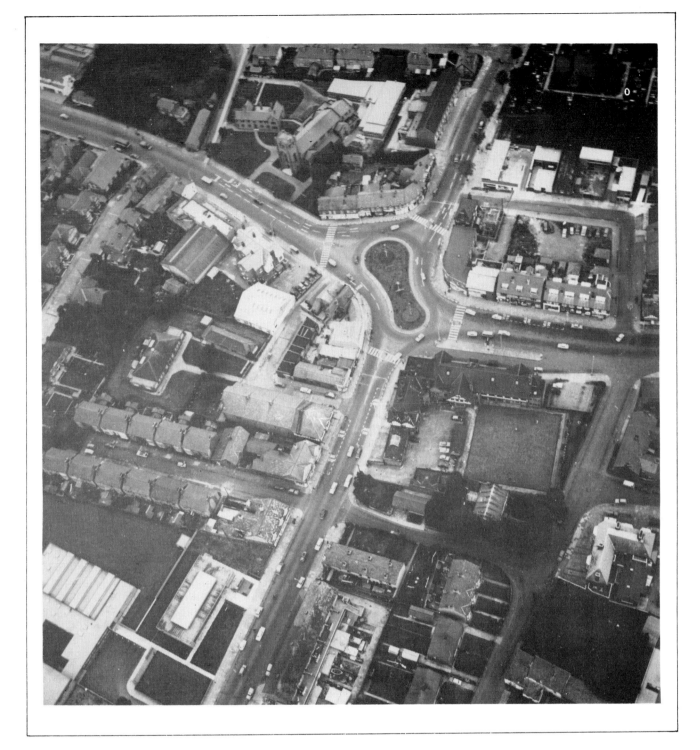

In this picture taken in 1962 (38 years later) there is only one farm left in Moreton, that is Stanley's farm on the corner of Sandbrook Lane, which was soon to be pulled down and replaced by Council flats. Old Hall Farm has become the headquarters of the Imperial Window Cleaning Company. Of Briscoe's farm, on the corner of Barnston Lane and Garden Lane, only the house remains, that was soon to go with the bowling green belonging to the Coach & Horses, and become Lennon's now Gateway's supermarket and car park. There are over 50 cars in this picture.

The top picture shows a shop on the corner of Chadwick Street about 1950. It was owned by Misses Lilian & Summerfield until Mr. Hopkins, standing on the step of his shop in the picture above, took over in 1947. The line of shops were pulled down in the middle 1960's. Mr. Hopkins then moved to Upton Road. The line of shops ran from Chadwick Street to the present day Co-operative shop on Hoylake Road. The other shops were — a fish shop, a habadashery shop and a chandler's shop, owned by Mr. Whitthread.

Below is the "Edgerley Cafe" built in the early 1900's with the houses going up the hill on a field of corn. At the present time two are empty, four have been pulled down (during the 1970's) and the others are being used by Solicitors and an Estate Agent. The lady standing in the front door of the Cafe is Miss Knowles. The Cafe later became the Co-operative shop, but is now the Golden Sunrise Take-away.

The top picture is of Miss Birch's shop. It was situated on the corner of Pasture Road and Moreton Cross just about where the zebra crossing is now. You had to go down a couple of steps to enter the shop and as a result it used to flood when it rained heavily, mainly in the winter.

The picture below, taken in the 1930's, is of Johnson's Electrical shop. It was situated in Chadwick Street and the building is still there. It was taken over by Boots Chemist and was used as a store room. It is now owned by the Abbey National Building Society. The name of the man standing in the doorway is Mr. Johnson.

Moreton Church of England School was built in 1861 and pulled down in 1973. The land was given by J.R. Shaw of Arrowe Hall. The plans were drawn up by J. Hay on the 10th May 1860 and approved by J. Thomas, Mr. Graham and W. Inman, the Shipping Magnate. The building was done by J. Thomas of Oxton at a cost of £745 and was opened on the 21st February 1861. The bricks that were used to build the school were hand-made, from a marl pit on the Meols Stretch, near to the present day Dog Kennels. The first head was Miss Ruth Dixon from Cumberland, who arrived on the 7th February 1861. She was 25 years old and stayed 27 years. The school was enlarged in 1864 and again in 1906, as can be seen in the photograph above and top right. The picture above, with the bell tower on the end of the building, dates from 1900, while the one on the top right, with the bell tower in the middle, dates from the 1910's. The card, bottom right, is the reverse of the one above. It shows Mrs. Hughes, the headmistress, ordering coal from the Wigan Coal Company at Upton Station. The old school closed in the summer of 1973, never to open again. The teachers and children moved to the Upton Road School. The last Head of the school was Mr. J. Appleyard.

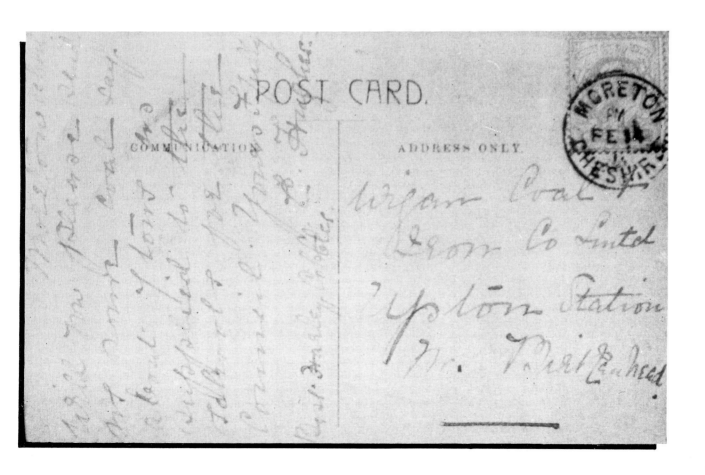

The picture above, dating from 1895, shows the field that ran down the left-hand side of the school and was used to grow vegetables to feed the school children. The field was where A.T. May (Travel Agents) and the other shops in that row are now.

The bottom picture shows a class of pupils, Mrs. Hughes, the Headmistress, is on the right of the picture, which dates from 1890.

The pictures on this page are of a more recent origin, the top one dates from 1973 showing the last pupil looking back as she leaves the school before it closes and moves to Upton Road.

Below shows the school being pulled down in 1975.

The two pictures on the left hand page show the first three shops built for Tich Mason in 1901. If you look between the upstairs windows you will see sandstone plaques with names on them, these are the names of horses that Tich Mason rode as winners in horse races and he used the money to build these shops. To-day the first shop is a Pet Shop, the second one a Butcher's and the third one a sweet shop. When they were first opened, the first one was rented by Jasper Byrom as a cycle shop, the second one by a Mr. Davenport who was a butcher and it has always been a butcher's shop, even to the present day. The third shop was a fish shop. At the back of the shops was a small abattoir, it was used to kill locally bought meat and was last used in the early 1920's. It was also used for a short time by the Post Office as a Sorting Office for local mail. It is now used as a garage-workshop (see picture below).

CHESHIRE FIELD COY
R.E. (TERRITORIALS) AT LEASOWE
APPROACHING LIGHTHOUSE. (1)
G.E. MILLS
L'POOL. N.

All four pictures on these pages were taken in 1910, they show the Birkenhead Territorials (Cheshire Field Coy R.E.) doing their training. They came to Moreton Shore every Whit week-end until after the First World War (1918). There was a rifle range at the junction of Leasowe Road/Pasture Road. It was used until the First World War and lead bullets can still be found dating from that period.

TERRITORIALS AT LEASOWE (4)
JUNE 1910
G.E. MILLS
L'POOL

B'HEAD TERRITORIALS AT LEASOWE G.E. MILLS
CAPT FORDE ON BRIDGE L'POOL N

BIRKENHEAD TERRITORIALS AT
LEASOWE JUNE 11 1910 (5) G.E. MILLS.
L'POOL. N.

MORETON HIGH SCHOOL.

RECORD SUCCESSES.

In the Faculty of Commerce Shorthand Examination (Gregg), six Certificates with Distinction have been awarded to the followng:—Marcus Gamble, Leslie Bridge, Mary Teasdale, Betty Teasdale (Elementary Grade), Hilda Andrews (Intermediate), Hilda Andrews (Advanced). There were six entries and six certificates were obtained. Also Leslie Bridge obtained a First Class Certificate (London College of Music) for Violin playing (Elementary).

Moreton High School was founded on Empire Day 1924 and closed in the early 1930's. The two buildings you see in the pictures still exist. The one on the left is the bungalow at No. 30 Joan Avenue and is called the Old School House. The one on the right is in Digg Lane; it is divided into flats and looks as though it has been built back to front, but in fact it is the right way round, the front facing the playing fields that were betweent two buildings. The School acquired a good repuation in its short life. It had its own magazine, seen on the right, and was also mentioned in the local papers.

Moreton High School (below) — **Back Row:** 1. Mrs. Andrews, 2. Phyllis Cormack, 3. Mary Teasdale, 4. Betty Teasdale, 5. (unknown), 6. Hilda Andrews, 7. Les Bridge, 8. Johnny Graham, 9. (unknown), 10. Graham Haldane, 11. Marcus Gamble, 12. Jerry Burden, 13. Jessie Hall, 14. Thelma Coldron, 15. Jenny Dodd, 16. Sonia Green, 17. D.G. Webster.
Middle Row: 1. Alma Walker, 2. Olive Day, 3. May Day, 4. (unknown), 5. (unknown), 6. (unknown), 7. Justin McCarthy?, 8. (unknown), 9. Justin McCarthy?, 10. Ronnie Kirkman, 11. (unknown), 12. Fred Pizzey, 13. Harold Darbyshire, 14. Stan Bridge.
Sitting on floor: 1. Dorothy Haygarth, 2. Joan Andrews, 3. (unknown), 4. Valerie Green, 5. (unknown), 6. Eunice Shaw?, 7. Betty Wilson?

Moreton High School 1928

Back row: (left to right) 1. D.G. Webster, 2. Phyllis Cormack, 5. Marcus Gamble, 6. Les Bridge, 7. Gerry Burden, 8. John Kirkman, 9. Johnny Graham, 10. Ronnie Kirkman.
Middle row: 2. Thelma Coldron, 1. Margaret Andrews, 3. ? Ray. 4. Billy Haygarth, 6. Sonia Green, 7. Jenny Dodd, 8. Jessie Hall, 9. Joan Andrews, 10. Alma Walker, 12. Stan Bridge, 13. Dorothy Haygarth.
Front row: 4. May Day, 5. Olive Day.

The top picture is of Pasture Road in 1910, looking to Moreton Shore. The building on the right is just before the Cadbury bungalow on Pasture Road. The bungalows were condemned in the 1930's and pulled down soon after.

The bottom picture was taken in the late 1920's. Pasture Road Farm is on the right. The shops were situated by the River Birket bridge and were also condemned and pulled down in the 1930's.

The picture above is of Pasture Road during the 1900's. The big house on the right of the picture was known as Father Berry's Holiday Home for Boys, built about 1900. It is still standing and is now a cafe called "Castle Blake", it was built originally to be used as a public house but was refused a licence. It was named after another horse that Tich Mason rode as a winner.

The picture below is of Pasture Road in the late 1920's looking to Moreton Shore. The bus in the distance is a Birkenhead one, probably a No. 77.

The Palais de Danse was built in the early 1900's from Army huts and was owned by Mrs. Oborn. It has been many things over the years; firstly a dance hall, then a roller skating rink and during the last war, it was used as a Community kitchen, returning to a skating rink after the war was over. Then in the middle 1960's it became the Labour Club, later changing to the Apollo Club, which it still is. The house adjoining the Club was originally a farmhouse, the people who lived there moved out in the late 1960's, and it then fell into a bad state of repair and was pulled down in 1988. The small building that can be seen on the side of the house was an Amusement Arcade which was last used in the early 1960's.

The picture above is of Leasowe Road, looking from the top of Reeds Lane towards Leasowe Children's Hospital. The picture dates from 1930 when Wallasey Council was in the process of putting in drains (see on the right of the picture), and up-grading the road. The picture, top right, was taken in the late 1930's. On the right of the picture is a concrete telephone box — there were very few of this type made. It was taken away and replaced with a red one, when the telephone box was moved to its present site in the 1950's. The Leasowe Castle Buffet, on the left of the picture, was built in 1890 for the Griffiths family as a holiday home (they were fish dealers from Liverpool). The Buffet changed hands several times, until it became a Cafe and Post Office. See picture below taken in the 1920's. It was closed during the war and used as a store house for fertilizers. It was opened again in 1950 by Mr. Jack Yue as a Chinese cafe. It closed its doors five years later and was pulled down. The site stayed vacant until the 1960's when a petrol station was built for B.P. It is now owned by Texaco.

LEASOWE ROAD, LEASOWE.

S. J. CARTER   LEASOWECASTLE   BUFFET   N° WALLASE

The top picture is of Gardenside/Leasowe Road in 1942/43. There is an air raid shelter on the left and in Gardenside there is an old bus shelter, which was one of four. The others were at Wakefield Drive, Leasowe Castle and Moreton Shore. The last one to be taken away was the one at Leasowe Castle in the late 1960's.

The picture below is of Reeds Farm, Leasowe. It stood where Farmside is now, just off Birket Avenue. The Sutton family lived on the farm and worked it.

Long Acre Cottage was built in 1815 and pulled down in 1934 by the Council. It was built by the Smith family and stood on a rectangular piece of land between Birket Avenue and Blackheath Drive. It had an earth floor to start with, later the Vyner family put in a wooden floor and added an extension to the right-hand side and charged the Smith family a rent for the work done. One of their children was very bright and Lord & Lady Cust paid for his education. The first picture is reputedly of Lord & Lady Cust visiting the cottage to check on the boy's progress. In the picture below, taken in 1934 just before it was pulled down, shows Mr. & Mrs. Brown, co-authors of the "Rise and Progress of Wallasey".

Leasowe Lighthouse was built in 1763 and is the oldest lighthouse in England. There were originally two lighthouses, the other one was a quarter of a mile out to sea on the other side of the embankment. It was washed away during a storm in 1769 and was replaced by one on Bidston Hill in 1771. Vessels coming home would line up the two lights and would then be able to enter the Rock Channel or the Hoyle Lake for safe anchorage. Leasowe Lighthouse was last used on the 15th July 1908 (see right-hand page). It was built with 660,000 hand-made bricks. The bricks were made on-site leaving a pond (see right-hand page) where the two boys are standing on the edge of it. It was filled in in the 1930's after two children drowned in it. In the early 1890's Mr. & Mrs. Williams were appointed to look after the Leasowe Lighthouse, having come from the Great Orme, Llandudno. Within a short time of their arrival Mr. Williams fell ill, and later died. Mrs. Williams had done such a good job, that when she asked if she could carry on with the job, the Mersey Docks and Harbour Board said yes. Mrs. Williams became famous and was mentioned in several of the newspapers of the day, she died in 1935. She had 13 children, the last one (Dolly) was the only one to be born at Leasowe Lighthouse — she died in Hoylake in 1990, aged 97. The picture below shows Mrs. Williams with four of her children. They are Dolly, Mrs. Williams, Aggie, Bertha and Eva. The lady on the left of the picture was their dressmaker.

OLD LIGHTHOUSE, LEASOWE, MORETON.

Mrm. 27.

Mersey Docks and Harbour Board.

NOTICE TO MARINERS.

LIGHTS AT
LEASOWE AND HOYLAKE LIGHTHOUSES.

NOTICE IS HEREBY GIVEN,
that the Fixed White Lights
now shewn from the Light-
houses at Leasowe and
Hoylake, will be discontinued
after sunrise of the 15th of
July, 1908.

BY ORDER,
MILES KIRK BURTON.
DOCK OFFICE.
Liverpool, May 28th, 1908.
General Manager and Secretary.

The picture on the right dates from 1910. The side buildings were used for storage and the one with double doors was a Coach House. The Coach House was used as a theatre on Sundays and the performers came from the Argyle Theatre in Birkenhead as it was closed on Sundays. After the show a hat was handed round for a collection. The picture below, showing the plans of the ground floor and outhouses, dates from 1928. The last family to live in the lighthouse was the Austin family and they left in 1929. It was put up for sale that year, but no one showed any interest. The Wallasey Council bought it in 1930 for £900 but it soon fell into disrepair and the outbuildings were pulled down, the windows bricked up and the door padlocked. It has been given a new lease of life lately, and when money allows, it will have the cast iron stairs replaced and will be open to the public. It is used as a Rangers' Office at the moment.

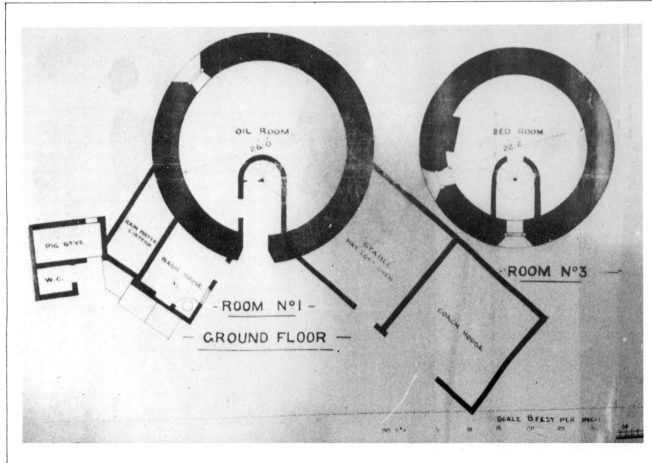

The picture above is of Carr Hall Farm; it was situated on the corner of Carr Lane/Hoylake Road, and was pulled down in the 1960's. The picture shows the original cottage with the Smith family standing outside; their names, from left to right are: Father — Ernest Smith with son Joseph in his arms, Cousins — Jack & Martha Edwards, and Mrs. Edwards and daughter Sally. The cottage was built in the last part of the 1790's and was later enlarged by incorporating the cottage into the house below in the 1920's. The quite large front garden was to disappear in the 1930's when the road was widened, the front door then opened onto the pavement.

Moreton Ladies Golf Club.

48

MORETON LADIES' GOLF CLUB.

Founded February, 1894.

Captain :
Miss A. A. Laird.

Hon. Treasurer :
Miss E. M. Smyth.

ELECTED TO THE L.G.U. 13th MARCH 1896

COMPETITION WINNERS.

Bowl presented by Miss Dod, to be held for six months.
Miss G. Cogswell.

Putting Competition, Miss K. Ball.

Bogey Competition, Mrs. Ryder Richardson.

Approach Shot, Miss Evans.

Mixed Foursomes, Miss Laird and Mr. J. Graham.

Open Competition Scratch Prize, May, 1896—1st, Miss M. E. Phillips (Wimbledon), 79 ; 2nd, Miss Issette Pearson (Wimbledon), 81.

Handicap Prize—1st, Miss Nimmo ; 2nd, Miss Frere.

Winner of prize competed for by winners of six Monthly Medals,
Miss W. Jackson.

Course :

1st hole.—200 yds., ditch to be carried from tee.

2nd hole.—140 yards, bunker about 50 yards in front of tee, ditch to catch ball running to hard over green.

3rd hole.—150 yards, ditch in front of tee, bunker 120 yards from tee guarding green.

4th hole.—280 yards, whins in front of tee, bunker about 90 yards from tee.

5th hole.—160 yards, whins in front of tee, 2 bunkers guarding green, ditch and bad ground beyond green.

6th hole.—210 yards, bunker 40 yards in front of tee, and bunker guarding green, rough ground off the line.

7th hole.—230 yards, bunker guarding green, rough ground on either side of course.

8th hole.—120 yards, bunker guarding green, ditch to catch pulled ball

9th hole.—110 yards, bunker just short of green, which is in a corner surrounded on 3 sides by hedge and ditch, ball over hedge out of bounds.

Record :

79 made by Miss M. E. Phillips, May, 1896.

Scratch and Bogey Scores 84.

Club Colours :

Red, black and yellow.

Entrance Fee and Subscription :

Entrance Fee, £3 2s. ; Annual Subscription, £1 1s.

Fixtures :

Spring Meeting, May.

Medal Day, second Wednesday in month.

Station :

1 mile from Moreton, on Wirral railway.

Moreton Ladies Golf Club was founded in February 1894. The Club House was situated on the corner of Lingham Lane and the Shore Road where a bungalow now stands. It was pulled down in the early 1950's. The leading ladies of the day were all members. Mrs. J.M. Laird and her three daughters, Mrs. Hudson of Hudson's Soaps, and the two greatest lady golfers of the day, Miss Graham who was the British champion in 1903 and Lottie Dod who was champion in 1904 Miss Dod also won the ladies singles tennis championship at Wimbledon, three times, and is still the youngest to have done so. The Golf Course consisted of nine holes going from Lingham Lane to Dovepoint, Meols, and back. It finally closed in 1914. The man in the top picture is probably John Ball, Jnr., who was the Professional.

The two pictures on this page are of Barnston Lane, it was originally called Chapel Lane. In the picture above, the boy standing at the front of the horse was known as little Harry Jones and lived in Dove Farm.

In the picture below, the white-fronted building at the end of Dial Terrace, was once a Wesleyan Chapel and was pulled down in the early 1960's.

Gorse Lane	—	Burnley Road
Glebe Road	—	Glebelands Road
Durban Road	—	Carnsdale Road
Cecil Avenue	—	Griffin Avenue
Hawthorn Avenue	—	Orchard Road
Park Road	—	Knutsford Road
Rossley Drive North	—	Rosslyn Drive
Stretton Drive	—	Dawpool Drive
Grafton Drive	—	Seaforth Drive
Oakland Drive	—	Cartmel Drive
Alexander Drive	—	Briscoe Drive
Newland Drive	—	Raby Drive
Churchill Road	—	Borrowdale Road
Hillcrest Avenue	—	Childwall Avenue
Woodland Road	—	Cobham Road
Northbrook Road	—	Westbrook Road
Birket Road	—	Broster Avenue
Grange Avenue	—	Garrick Avenue
Smithy Lane	—	Netherton Road
Chapel Lane	—	Barnston Lane
Station Road	—	Pasture Road
Birkenhead Road Main Road	—	Hoylake Road
Mary Ann's Lane	—	Old Maryland Lane
Cross Lane	—	Ditton Lane
Stanton Road	—	Willaston Road

The majority of road names in Moreton were different to those of to-day — the reason why this came about was the take-over of Moreton by Wallasey in 1928, and later Saughall Massie in 1933, many of the names were the same or similar to those in Wallasey. This was not the main reason, Wallasey also tried to call Moreton — West Wallasey and there were no A to Z's in those days. Opposite is a list of names — old and present day.

On the next 2 pages there is a map of Moreton and Saughall Massie, made just before the take-over by Wallasey.

Nineteen Questions
In and About Moreton

1. What stood at the corner of Smithy Lane
   Of fair repute and honest name,
   Long gone of course — for in its place
   Stands a successor of handsome grace.
   A mellowed fount of tasteful charms.
   It was the original 'Farmers' Arms'.

2. Founded firmly upon bales of cotton
   Though presently neglected — almost forgotten
   Once it played quite a vital role
   In saving the imperiled mariner's sole.
   The answer comes easy to those with nouse
   It is our ancient now disused lighthouse

3. What rural district abutting our shore
   Had residents but numbering four
   Long at rest neath Christ Church sod
   Peter — Jack — Stan and Maggie Dodd.
   Would quickly inform if you could ring 'em
   It is none other than lonely Lingham.

4. Before Moreton publically displayed time
   What in an earlier, gentler clime
   Had enclosed by walled surrounding
   A plantation with great trees abounding.
   Old locals will be at no loss
   They'll remember it was Moreton Cross

5. On rising ground above Arrowes Rill
   Where formerly stood Saughall Massie Mill
   What had a front gate — shaped as a ship's wheel
   Larger it seemd that would have been real.
   A mansion – cosied as only money could arrange
   It was, of course, Saughall Massie Grange

6. Barring the road twixt Hoylake and Town
   For vehicular traffic — both up and down
   What in Saughall Massies younger day
   Stood at the juncture of Garden Hey.
   Until it suffered the Dodo's sad fate
   It was, of course, the Toll Bar Gate

7. What before the mid-twenties while
   Before was built the Cathedrals pile
   Before was destroyed the White Cottage Row
   Abutting the road the shoreward does go.
   What name had the Forum – where friend met friend
   Old locals gathered there – 'Carthouse End'.

8. What onetime creation of Topiarian Art
   In Moreton's "diadem" played notable part
   Presently perpetuated upon an opposite site
   It there affords beveraged delight.
   Old 'Gamp' Smith attended it there
   It was, of course, his old Armchair

9. What old Moreton house — (old is the clue)
   Had stables — shippons and pigsties too
   A barn, and lofts in plentiful profusion
   Plus a cobbled yard to complete the illusion.
   With never a field or rickyards charm
   It was – it is – Old Hall Farm

10. An oasis where animals could partake
    Cooling draughts their thirsts to slake
    What feature lay in days prewar
    Beside the road leading to the Shore.
    Old locals – they have the gist of it
    It was the wayside watering pit

11. Before Wallasey's destructive pillage
    Which tore rusticity from our village
    What was the name of the laneway there
    Which runs beside the "Farmers" here.
    Barnston now – I tell you plain
    Originally it was Chapel Lane

12. What name had the Chapel Lane Farm
    A pleasant place of redbricked charm
    Which commemorated for a great long while
    A monkish columbrariums pile.
    Unless with ignorance you are hand in glove
    You will know it was the Farm of Dove

13. What stood opposite the narrow lane
    That took title from the Sandbrooks name
    Worked by the Rimmers — Jack and Fred
    It had no chestnut trees outspread.
    Companioned by a stunted withy
    It was the late lamented Village Smithy

14. What name had the picturesque cot
    Which nestled in a cosy spot
    Beside a yet rural Town-Meadow-Lane
    To-day its perpetuated in a Closes name.
    I tell you truly without least duplicity
    Most aptly named – it was Felicity.

15. In Pasture Roads nearby region
    Directly opposite the Royal British Legion
    What old lane was totally destroyed
    When adjoining lands were urbanly employed.
    Picturesque – without other claim to fame
    It was none other than Old Clap Lane

16. A revered relic of far yesterday
    Its outstretched arms silhouetted grey
    What on the way to Birkenhead Town
    Caps woodland slopes like a crown.
    There upstanding upon its hill
    It is – what else – Bidston Hill

17. After fruitful years of voyaging free
    Around and about Mersey's Estuary
    What ship — driven by seas wild booming
    Lay long decades in embankment tombing.
    Locals their manner quite emphatic
    Will tell it was the Hoylake Smack 'Emblematic'

18. What once stood above the grassy cop
    Which crowned Leasowe Embankment top
    For decades there without dispute
    Commemorating the deed of one Canute.
    Of giant size unadorned and bare
    It was Leasowe's pseudo 'Canutes Chair'

19. What was the one-time horse-racing course
    Where thieves — rogues and others worse
    Schemed and plotted in furtive places
    To contrive winners for the Races.
    A'top Sandbrook Lane amid woodlands dark
    The Courses name it was 'Upton Park'.

These two pictures are of Mary Ann's Lane, now Old Maryland Lane. Both pictures were taken in 1909. Mary Ann is standing on the left in the top picture and Dove Farm and Dove Cottage are in the background on the right, and were pulled down in the early 1960's. The foundations of May Ann's cottage can still be found in the grounds of the Gospel Hall.

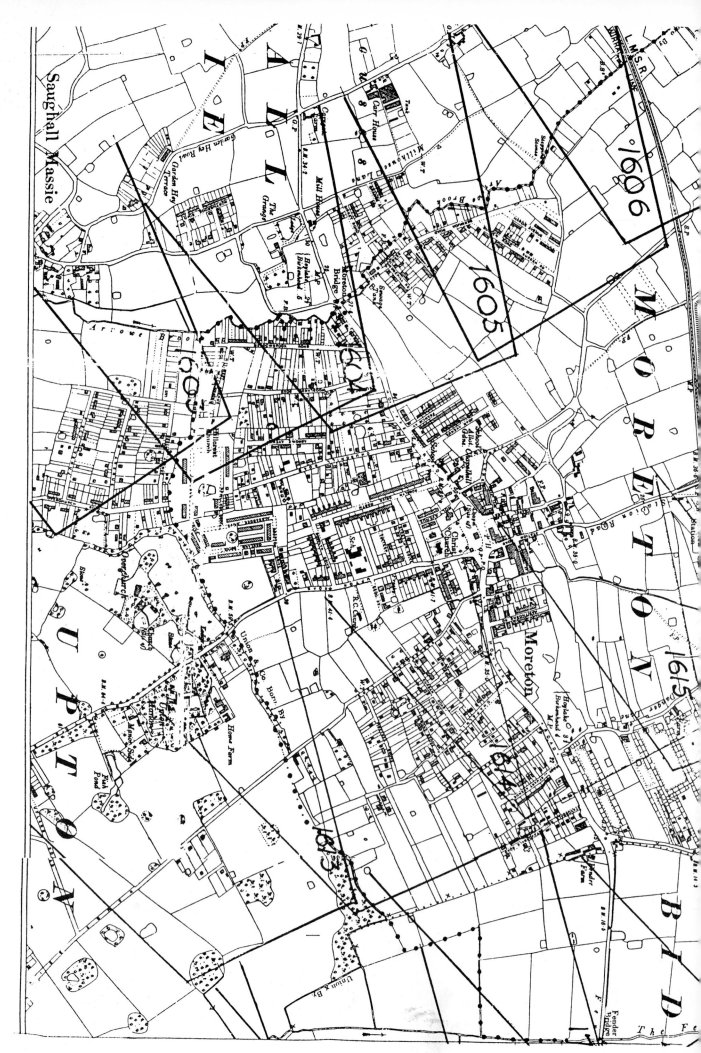

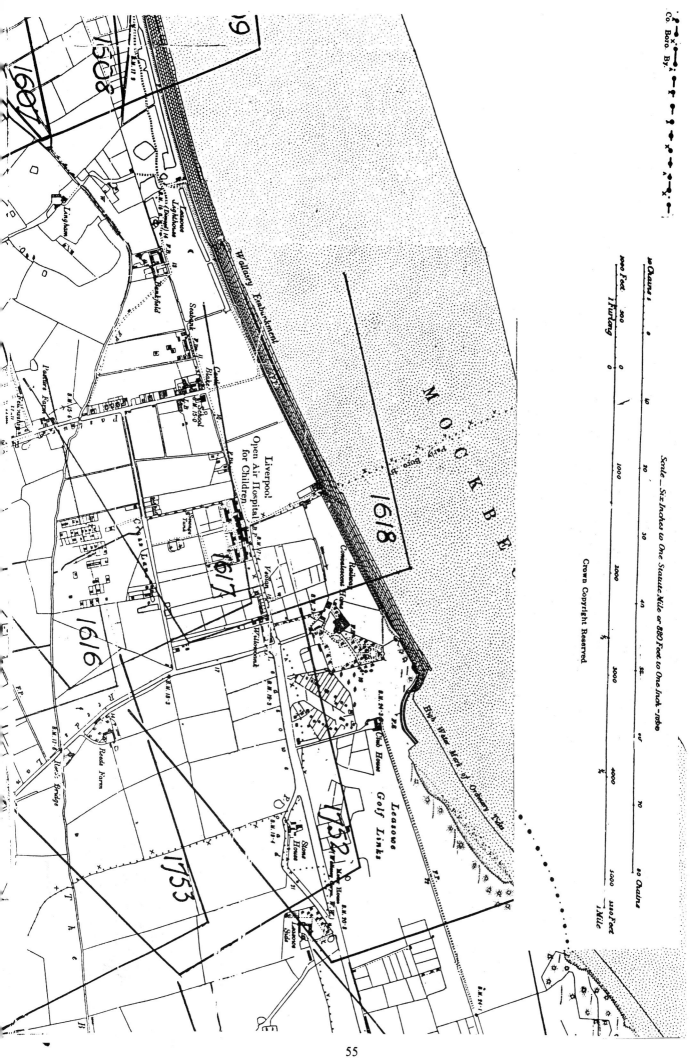

Job Thomas, the Bakers, was built about 1845 and pulled down in the early 1980's. In the top picture, taken about 1900, you can see Mr. Thomas holding the horse; he bought most of his produce from the local farms. He moved to the corner of Silverburn Avenue in the early 1900's, and was there until the early 1960's. His old shop was then converted into a house; if you look in the picture below, and on the facing page, you can see the different coloured bricks, indicating the old shop front. In the picture below you can see Mr. Mortimer's shop, and in the extreme left of the picture, you can just make out Danny Evans' shop. These shops were all pulled down in 1973, to be replaced by Boots Chemist, Rumblelows and the carpet shop, with the Solicitors above.

Job Thomas's old house, just before it was pulled down in the early 1980's. The last person to live in the house was Miss Thomas. The space at the back of the building was used to sell second-hand furniture by Mr. Storey.

Below are the present day shops that replaced the buildings, built in 1989, owned by R.H. Jones & Chapman.

The picture above is of the Moreton Railway Company bridge on Pasture Road when it was being widened in 1935/36. On the left of the picture, you can see H. Hough & Co. Ltd., the timber merchants, who were there until the late 1960's when they closed their yard down.

Below is Station Approach in 1909 when it was a bad winter. The man in the picture is Mr. Joseph Bell, Senior, the Moreton Station Master.

The top picture dates from 1925 showing the site where Cadburys (now Premier Brands — "A" Block) is situated, the site was known as Birds Field.

The picture below, dating from 1927, showing the Marina Cafe and the building with the telegraph pole outside, is now the main entrance to the factory. The buildings were pulled down in 1935 after being condemned.

MANNING'S CORNER, MAIN RD, MORETON.

Both these pictures date from the 1930's. The top picture shows Mannings Newsagents, on the corner of Chapelhill Road; which is now owned and run by Mr. & Mrs. Timperley.

The picture below shows Hoylake Road, with Chapelhill Road on the left; of the three buildings in the picture, the cottage is the only one not now standing, having been pulled down in 1947 to widen the road and build the present day houses. The bungalow in the middle of the picture, was built for a Captain Chamberlain in the 1920's.

ANCIENT & MODERN, HOYLAKE RD, MORETON

Both these pictures were taken about 1900 from approximately where Netherton Road is now. The top picture shows Churchill Farm on the right, now Holt Avenue. The cottage in the middle is where the present day Co-operative shop is now on Hoylake Road. The bottom picture is facing Chadwick Street (the only 'street' in Moreton). The haystack on the left of the picture, stands where the Abbey National Bank and Baxter's (Butchers) stand now. The planks of wood and building material in the bottom picture, are for the building of the Sunrise Cafe.

Both pictures are of Hoylake Road about 1903/4. The top picture is looking towards Moreton Cross and the bottom one towards Birkenhead. The cart is taking school children home after a heavy downpour of rain flooded the road opposite the present Catholic Church. The road still floods now after heavy rain.

The top picture was taken in 1904. It shows the corner of Sandbrook Lane and the house on the right was moved in the early 1920's. The two men with scythes were going to cut hay; behind them is the entrance to Stanley's farm. The picture below is also of Sandbrook Lane with Glebelands Road in the background and Smith's farm on the right. The two cows are drinking out of the River Sandbrook. The river is still there, but is now drained off into the drainage system. The picture was taken in 1927.

The above picture of the house was taken in 1929. The house was built about 1900 and the two people standing in the doorway are Mrs. Knowles and her son Eric. The house still stands and is now occupied by the Wirral Spark Plug Company.

Below is Poston's Garage, built approximately 1920, and is next door to the house in the picture above. This garage replaced three terraced cottages. The three men from left to right are: Jack Whatling, Jack Knowles and Gerard Poston. On the roll-door above is an advertisement for Chester Races 4/6d and 6/-d on Cup Day. The building presently houses the 'Olde World' furniture shop.

The picture above, taken in 1987, shows little has changed other than the use of buildings. Below is the Smithy which was down the side of the Car Shop. It was in use until middle 1950's and finally closed through the lack of horses in the area. The men in the picture, from left to right are: Jack Peers, Thomas Mutch, Jack Rimmer, Albert Parkinson, Frederick Jackson Rimmer and William Jebson Rimmer. The four men with aprons on were wheelwrights.

Moreton Village

The top picture is of Moreton Cross with Upton Road on the left, taken in 1914. Three more shops were added by Tich Mason in 1911, to the ones which were already built, see page 30. These shops are still standing and are occupied by M.S.A., a television shop, Wirral Estate Agents and Max Spielman's. Church Farm, on the right of the shops in the top picture, was pulled down about 1929, and was replaced by the District Bank, which is now the National Westminster Bank. The picture below is of a group of local men standing with their backs to Church Farm's farmyard. The wooden fence was put there to stop people looking over the wall. The names of the men in the picture are, from left to right:— T. Stanley, B. Tarrant, S. Massey, J. Stanley (Sprat), F. Mountain, H. Clarke, A. Stanley, G. Smith, B. Smith, D. Stanley, J. Harty and E. Mutch.

These two pictures are of the British Legion Gala Day in 1927 shortly after the Plantation was taken away. In the top picture, on the left, is a Crosville bus outside the old Coach & Horses public house. On the right of the terrace cottages is the old District Bank, which was the first bank in Moreton. It opened on the 8th May 1919 and its name was 'Manchester & Liverpool District Banking Company', and later in 1924 its name was shortened to 'District Bank'. The bank moved in 1930 to a purpose built bank on the corner of Chadwick Street, see left-hand page.

The two pictures on this page are of the Plantation at Moreton Cross. The top picture dates from 1900 — the children belong to the Stanley family. The bottom picture dates from 1912. The building on the left is of the Plough Inn. The Plantation was used by the police as a Pinfold to put stray cows and sheep in. The Plantation was cleared of all trees in 1926 with the exception of one tree, a silver birch, see top picture on facing page.

The top picture is of Moreton Cross in 1926 — just after the trees were taken down on the Plantation. Mr. Greeny's shop is on the right. It was later to become Strothers (now Rumbelows), which is now part of Lloyd's Bank. The side wall of the bank is where the haridressers and cobbler's shops are now. The picture below shows Moreton Cross looking up Hoylake Road towards Birkenhead. The lamp post and sign post on the right of the picture, marks where the roundabout was. It was also used as a bus stop, this dates from 1929. The lamp post replaced the three that was blown down in 1927.

The top picture of Pasture Road (originally Station Road) was taken about 1903. The white terrace cottages were known as Herring Row; the name came about because the fishermen cured herrings in the old farm buildings at the back. This did not last long as the people in the cottages objected. The building that was used could be seen in a painting which was in Moreton Library, until it was stolen in 1990. The cottages were pulled down soon after this picture was taken — two houses were built in their place, see the picture below. The were first used as a Maternity Home run by Nurse Dick and later they were changed into shops in the late 1930's. One shop is the Fish & Chip shop, then Moreton Mart and the other a Car Assessory shop. The sandstone and brick cottages on the left in the top picture, were built in the mid 1700's and pulled down in 1933 when the road was widened. Two of the last families to live in them were the Brassey and the Hazelhurst families. Moreton Library now stands on this site.

STATION RD. MORETON.

The two pictures on this page are again of (Station Road) Pasture Road. The top picture dates from 1909, the bottom one from the early 1920's. On the left of both pictures is a three story house; later in the 1920's it had an extension put on the front to accommodate three shops, see page 69. The small white wooden bungalow on the right in the top picture was the first Fish & Chip shop in Moreton. It was pulled down in 1919 and replaced by the Moreton Picture House which opened on the 30th April 1921 (it cost 9d in the front stalls). It closed on the 28th March 1964 to become a Bingo Hall, which it still is. The shop which can just be seen on the right of the picture was Lunt's Cake shop. It was later moved to the corner of Rosslyn Drive (in the late 1930's). The shop then became a Cafe until the early 1980's, and is now a mens' clothing shop called 'Michaels'.

THE VILLAGE MORETON

The picture at the top is of the Moreton pump that stood between the old Picture House (now the bingo hall) and the newsagents next door. The two people in the picture are Nellie Usher and Jack Gardiner — the picture dates about 1900. There was an old wives tale of witches nearby who put a spell on children who played with the pump and wasted water. The water that supplied the pump has been piped off into the street drains.

The picture below dates from 1911 and is of Pasture Road. On the left is Job Thomas and his family outside the shop they ran on the corner of Silverburn Avenue until the 1960's. They moved to this shop, from Hoylake Road/Digg Lane, see pages 56/58. The butcher's shop in the picture did not last long, it quickly became a newsagents, owned by Joseph Bell, senior. Later it was run by Barton Mills until the 1960's and is still a newsagents.

The picture at the top is of Garden Lane in the mid 1920's. The butcher's shop and Tarrant's Fish & Chip shop were extensions added in the late 1920's. The third shop was owned by the Cairns family and they sold childrens' clothes. The terrace was called Moreton Terrace and was built about the turn of the century and pulled down in the early 1970's. The end building in the top picture was three storey's high and the rest two storeys. In the 1930's when Pasture Road was widened, the three storey one was taken down and the rest were left — it is now a car park. The bottom picture was taken just before they were demolished in 1973.

The top picture is of Moreton Post Office and is now a Pet Shop. It has been many things from a furniture shop, cafe, grocer's, Army & Navy Stores and more. The people in the picture are, from left to right: Mrs. Agnes Roberts (an aunt), one of the cousins Fred Watling, a local girl, and almost out of the picture Ernest Watling (their father), who also ran the Post Office. The picture dates from 1904.

The bottom picture shows the Post Office van used for the collection and delivery of mail. The Postman Driver was Alex Parry. The picture dates from the 1920's.

The Midland Bank came to Moreton in the summer of 1919, becoming the second bank to do so. The District (now Nat West) Bank being the first by a short head. It was a sub branch of the Bank's Hoylake Branch. The Midland Bank's first premises were Stroud's Fish & Poultry shop, until the 1920's, when it moved to its present site at No. 200 Hoylake Road, it was later extended in 1966. Stroud's Fish & Poultry shop is at present a Gent's barbers shop. The picture below is showing A. Cobb's shop on the left and Rudkin's which was a fruit & fish shop. It was run like this until the 1950's. It is now a television shop. The names of the people, from right to left, are T. Rudkin (son — on the bike), Mr. Rudkin in the front of Mrs. Rudkin and their daughter Cissie, to the left.

The top picture is of Upton Road/Moreton Road where the spur road, leading to the motorway, is now. The picture shows the Lodge that belonged to Paul's mansion. The Lodge is falling down, having not been lived in for some years. The Mansion fell into a bad state of repair and was pulled down in the late 1940's-early 1950's. It was used as a Home for "bad girls" for a while before being left empty. The small estate that was built on the Scout's Field has the road named after the Paul family, they were Millers of flour on a large scale. The picture below again of Upton Road/Moreton Road looking toward Moreton Cross. The banner is indicating the entrance to Upton Park Race Course — it is now the spur to the motorway. The Race Course was owned and run by the Ahern family, it had a short life of six years, from 1922 to Easter 1928. The first race was run on the 15th April 1922. The land was sold to the Wallasey Corporation for use as a cemetery. It was never used for that purpose — Frankby Cemetery was used instead.

BERMUDA ROAD. MORETON.

Both these pictures are of Bermuda Road, taken about 1927/30. The road was not improved until 1932. Up to then there was only a wooden bridge across the River Arrowbrook in Bermuda Road, see bottom picture. In the winter, the coal cart used to get bogged down to the axle and the horse could not move it, so the men had to carry the coal halfway down the road until the horse could pull the wagon through the mud. The coal merchant was Mr. Bridge.

The top picture shows Smithy Lane now Netherton Road in the 1910's. There used to be a Smithy behind the Farmer's Arms until the 1930's when it closed.

Below is a view from Barnston Lane, approximately 1900. It was called Chapel Lane then and was changed when Wallasey took over Moreton, see page 51.

The picture above shows Barnston Lane before the first two houses were changed into shops. One was a bakery run by Penningtons, and is still a cake shop now. The other one was, and still is, a general shop. The picture below shows Barnston Lane with Old Hall Farm, on the left behind the trees. The Farm is the oldest building in Moreton dating from 1719 and was built for Daniel and Mary Wilson. On the right is Yew Tree Farm, which was pulled down in the 1950's. It was run by the Parkinson family who had several other farms in Moreton as there were three brothers who all wanted their own farm. The brother that ran Yew Tree Farm was known as "Bunker" Parkinson as he collected the waste from all the caravans.

Both pictures on this page are of the Mersey Dock & Harbour Board house, which was built for the Wall Engineer. It was originally a single storey building when first built in approximately 1840. It was extended upwards in 1896 to accommodate the large family living there, namely the Beed family. The lady in the picture on the left, is Mrs. Beed burning rubbish in the garden. The man wearing the bowler hat, in the bottom picture, is one of the M.D. & H.B. Directors, his chauffeur is behind him on the right. The building was pulled down in the late 1960's when it was known that the wall was going to be re-built.

SEA WALL, LEASOWE.

The top picture shows Pasture Road by the River Birket in 1924 after a storm had washed away the right hand side of the bridge. Two foot bridges were built, one on each side of the road for pedestrians, as the bridge could only take single line traffic.

The bottom picture was taken after a heavy rain fall in 1927. The car reputedly belonged to Tich Mason and the children came from the camp site on Kerr's field. The house belonged to Tich Mason and is still standing by the River Birket bridge on Pasture Road, it was built in 1900. Graham White, the famous aviator, was the owner before Tich Mason.

Leasowe from the Air.

The picture on the left is more like Pasture Road from the air, not Leasowe. At the bottom of the picture is Leasowe Road to the left. Shore Road is to the right. Looking to the top of the picture, on the right, is the River Birket. On the left, two thirds up, is Cross Lane now Ditton Lane, see page 86. This picture was taken in 1924.

The picture above and the one below were both taken from the top of the lighthouse. The top picture dates from 1911 when it was mainly tents that were used — it would be another 6 or 7 years before it changed to look like the bottom picture taken in the early 1930's. There were 2,000 plus holiday homes, caravans and chalets in and around Moreton. The bulk of them were at Moreton Shore on Kerr's Field.

The top picture was taken from the top of the lighthouse in 1988 (a big difference from the previous page) showing the last permanent caravan site at Moreton shore. The site is owned by an old Moreton family, The Biddles. They also run the last farm in Moreton.

Below is a picture of Moreton Common in 1925. The group of people in the middle are attending a Sports Day, possibly one of the last, as by the 1930's they had stopped — see pages 88 & 89.

The top picture is of Moreton Common showing two of the lagoons. These came about with the building of the first wall in 1822, the clay was dug out to form them. Later the wall was strengthened with sandstone taken from the Breck Quarry in Poulton. Parts of the wall survived until the modern wall was built in the 1970's when the lagoons were filled in. Below, shows the Love family — often the whole family stayed for the entire summer, some hardy ones stayed until November.

CROSS LANE, MORETON.

The top picture is of Cross Lane, now Ditton Lane, taken about 1914. On the right hand side, where the cows are, was the Christchurch Mission. The Mission was built because the population had grown so large. It was pulled down in the 1930's and moved to Barnston, and is now used as a church hall.

"CHRISTCHURCH MISSION" MORETON.

Cole's Bus Service was the first motorised bus service in Moreton. It was originally run from Moreton Station to Moreton Shore, then from Moreton Cross to the Shore when Birkenhead started their bus service to Moreton Cross in 1920; the Crosville followed in 1925. Wallasey started their bus service in 1928, the No. 4 bus was the one that serviced Moreton Shore, bringing the day trippers by the bus load from Seacombe Ferry. By then Cole's Bus Service had finished; it last ran in 1925. Mr. Cole is standing in front of the bus in both pictures. He and his family came to Moreton as campers and established "Cole's Camp Field" where Kingsmead Road is now.

Sports Day on Leasowe Common started in the early 1890's, in fact 1891, August Bank Holiday is reputed to be the first one — the first race was the under 5's Egg & Spoon Race. The organisation was on the haphazard side, until the turn of the century. By 1903 they had got sponsors for the prizes. The Mayor was one of the Patrons. An Hon. Secretary, President, Judges etc., had become highly organised with "a programme of events" costing 2d then, two pence now.

At the end of the day, there was a Dance — Entrance Fee 3d, children 1d. The dance was held at the City Caterers pavillion — 7.30 p.m. to 12 midnight. The music was supplied by Madame Clough's Band, the programme cost 6d. The Sports Day ceased in the 1930's as the caravans were moved. After being condemned by Wallasey Council (after the take-over of Moreton by Wallasey), the caravan holiday resort came to an end. Fifty happy years with happy memories for thousands of people who came from all over the country in its hay-day. Moreton was well known in its time and had a good reputation.

Floods in Moreton mainly happened because most of the land was, and still is, below sea level, so it was prone to flooding. People waded to Moreton Station in their wellingtons and then changed into their shoes before going on to the village. The two pictures are of Kerr's Field when it was flooded in August 1912 — nevertheless all the people had happy smiling faces.

The top picture on this page is again of Kerr's Field taken in 1918 when it was flooded. The bottom picture is also of Kerr's Field, this time dating from October 1927.

The two pictures on this page are of Shore Road during floods. The top picture is looking towards the lighthouse, dating from October 1927, and the one below is looking towards Pasture Road, dating about 1914.

Storms at Moreton have had a devastating effect in the past as the picture above shows; these happened during the autumn of that year. The picture below is of the last great flood — it happened in 1956 after a torrential downpour. The picture was taken from a window of one of the Hospital bungalows in Ditton Lane looking towards Cadbury's. Cadburys can be seen in the distance — the factory was only half built at the time.

The submerged forest that can be seen on the two pictures started just past the lighthouse and stretched along the coast to just beyond Dovepoint in Meols. The forest originally went out as far as 2½ miles, and probably joined up with its counterpart on the Liverpool side, namely Formby Point. It dates back at least 5,000 years and it is known that a graveyard was out there as a gravestone was found. Remnants of some kind of dwellings were found also tree stumps, as shown in the pictures. The tree stumps that are in the pictures were dated by Carbon Dating System to be 5,000 years old. The last remnants of the stumps disappeared in 1956 after a storm. There are still some peat beds but they are just a pale picture of the past. The top picture dates from the late !800's and the bottom one from the early 1900's.

Of the two pictures on this page, the top one is a printed postcard dating from December, 1904, and the bottom a photograph taken in the Spring of 1906. They tell the story of a Spanish ship that was carrying oranges into the Port of Liverpool. It was wrecked just off Leasowe Bay in a storm on the 8th December 1904. Its cargo of oranges was washed ashore in Leasowe Bay and later the ship itself came to rest there as can-be seen in the picture below. People came from miles around to get what they could, and as the oranges were packed in barrels, they took the barrels home and used them as water butts. The ship itself was quickly stripped of everything that was not nailed down.

The top postcard dates from the early 1920's when Birkenhead ran the only bus service to Moreton. The writing on the bus was put on the card after the picture was taken and used as an advertisement for the bus service.

The card below was the type where the town's name was left blank and could be added later, sometimes a rubber hand stamp was used. This card dates from the early 1920's.